ARTIST TRANSCRIPTIONS
TRUMPET

Miles Davis
Standards Volume 2

Cover Photo: Raymond Ross

ISBN 0-634-00557-X

HAL•LEONARD® CORPORATION

7777 W. BLUEMOUND RD. P.O. BOX 13819 MILWAUKEE, WI 53213

Visit Hal Leonard Online at
www.halleonard.com

Miles Davis
Standards Volume 2

Contents

4   *Biography*

5   *Discography*

6   Airegin

12   Basin Street Blues

17   Footprints

24   I'll Remember April

34   It Never Entered My Mind

36   Lament

31   Nature Boy

38   Oleo

43   'Round Midnight

46   Some Day My Prince Will Come (master)

50   Some Day My Prince Will Come (alternate take)

56   Stella By Starlight

53   What's New?

66   Will You Still Be Mine

76   Yesterdays

Biography

Miles Davis was one of the most important musicians in American music. An individual trumpet stylist, Miles Davis had more career highs than six giants of the music scene combined. He left many landmark recordings in a career that spanned bebop, cool jazz, modal jazz, fusion and hip-hop. He also promoted and discovered some of the most important musicians in the jazz world, including Bill Evans, John Coltrane, Red Garland, Chick Corea, Dave Liebman, Ron Carter, Wayne Shorter, and many, many others.

Miles Dewey Davis was born on May 25, 1926 in Alton, Illinois, but grew up in East St. Louis. He began playing trumpet when he was nine or ten. He went to New York in 1944 to study at the Juilliard School of Music, but he really wanted to be part of the jazz scene, so he dropped out after a few months. He played with Coleman Hawkins on recordings and gigs on 52nd Street, but by 1945 Miles was playing and recording with Charlie Parker. His style at that time was often tentative, but Parker and other musicians believed in him. Miles later gained valuable experience in the orchestra of Benny Carter on the West Coast, but he was back with Parker by 1948.

Miles took over a nine-piece rehearsal band with arrangements by Gerry Mulligan, Gil Evans, George Russell, John Lewis, and John Carisi in late 1948. It played one or two live gigs with varying personnel, but became famous as the "Birth of the Cool" ensemble based on twelve recordings for the Capitol label. These recordings highlighted a new approach to ensemble jazz and improvisation and continue to be influential.

Miles worked infrequently in the early '50s mainly due to a substance abuse problem, but he kicked the habit by 1954. An appearance at the Newport Jazz Festival in 1955 was a major success for him, and during this period he led a quintet featuring John Coltrane, Red Garland, Paul Chambers and Philly Joe Jones. Along with albums with this lineup which are now considered jazz classics, he began an association with composer/arranger Gil Evans that yielded several large orchestral albums garnering spectacular reviews and influencing players and composers worldwide.

In 1959, with an all-star ensemble of Coltrane, Chambers, Cannonball Adderley, Bill Evans, and Jimmy Cobb, Miles recorded the album *Kind of Blue*. This album became one of the most consistent selling albums in the history of the recording industry; it continues to be a top-selling catalog recording. The music on the album kick-started the modal jazz movement, and two of the five tunes became jazz standards.

By 1964, Davis was leading another incredible ensemble which included tenor saxophonist Wayne Shorter, keyboardist Herbie Hancock, bassist Ron Carter, and drummer Tony Williams. While still playing standard songs and new compositions, the group was looser and incorporated more modern and even avant-garde elements. The music continued to evolve, and by 1968, Davis encouraged the musicians to incorporate electronics and rock. Soon Chick Corea, bassist Dave Holland and drummer Jack DeJohnette were the featured players, and this ensemble was later known as one of the earliest 'fusion' ensembles. In fact, the double album *Bitches Brew* is cited as the recording that launched the fusion era of jazz. Long-time fans were confounded and alienated, but Miles pressed on in his new direction; his groups often included more than one guitar and/or keyboard. Miles was now controversial, and his live appearances were more popular with rock audiences than jazz fans. Ill health sidelined Davis in 1975, and for all intents and purposes, he'd retired. But in 1981, he was back with a group incorporating funk and modern pop music. One of the last concerts he played was a Quincy Jones-produced re-visit to the Birth of the Cool repertoire at the Montreux jazz festival. Miles died on September 28, 1991 in Santa Monica, California.

Miles Davis

Discography

Airegin, Oleo – LP: Prestige 7109; CD: OJC-245

Basin Street Blues – LP: Columbia; CD: Sony CK 48827

Footprints – LP: Columbia CL 9401; CD: Sony CK 65682

I'll Remember April – LP: Prestige 7054; CD: OJC-093

It Never Entered My Mind (from *Workin'*) – CD: JV 60126

Lament – LP: Columbia CL 1041; CD: Sony CK 65121

Nature Boy – LP: Debut 120; CD: OJC-043

'Round Midnight (from *Best*) – CD: JVCJ 60818

Some Day My Prince Will Come – LP: Columbia CL 1656; CD: Sony CK 65919

Stella By Starlight – CD: Sony CXK 66955

What's New? – LP: Prestige 7858; CD: Prestige 24117

Will You Still Be Mine – LP: Prestige 7352; CD: OJC-6017

Yesterdays (from *Young Man with a Horn*) – Classic Compact Jazz

AIREGIN

By SONNY ROLLINS

Fast

Intro
Sax

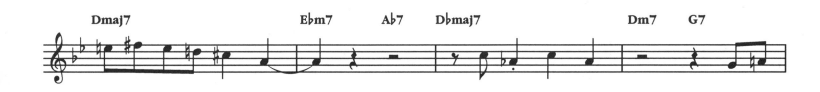

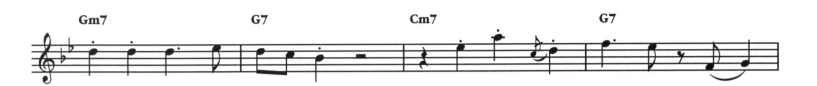

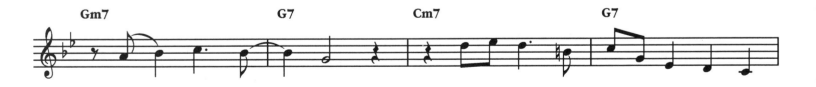

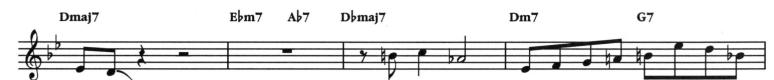

Sax Solo

BASIN STREET BLUES

Words and Music by
SPENCER WILLIAMS

Free time

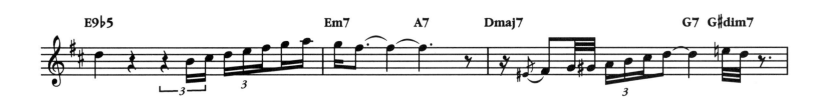

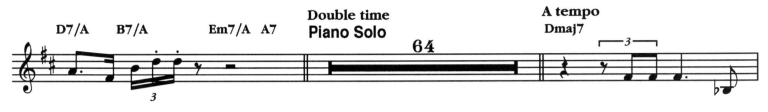

FOOTPRINTS

By WAYNE SHORTER

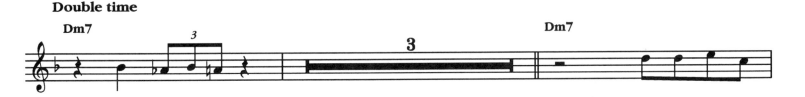

Double time

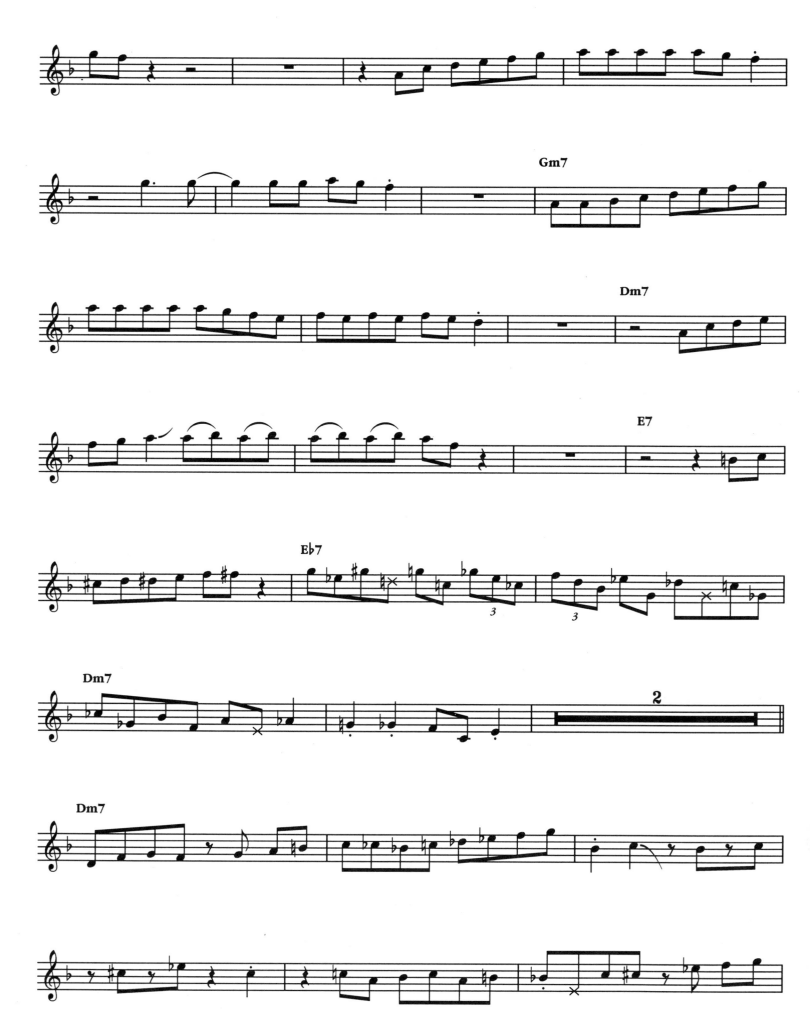

Gm7

Dm7

A tempo

E7   **Eb7**

Double time

Dm7   **Dm7**

2

Gm7

Dm7

A tempo

Double time

A tempo

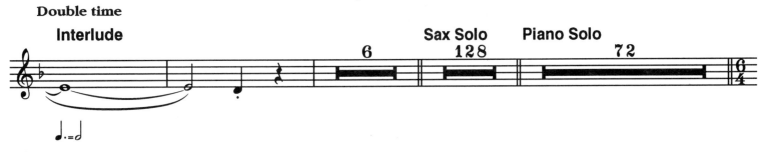

I'LL REMEMBER APRIL

Words and Music by PAT JOHNSON,
DON RAYE and GENE DE PAUL

Bm7

E7   C#m7   F#7   Bm7

E7   Amaj7   Dm7

G7   Cmaj7   Dm7

G7   Cmaj7   Bm7

E7   Amaj7

Abm7   Db7   Gbmaj7

Bm7   E7   Amaj7

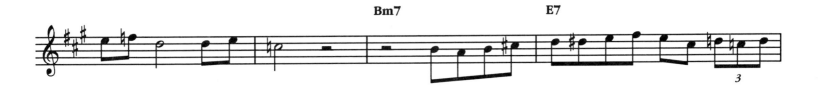

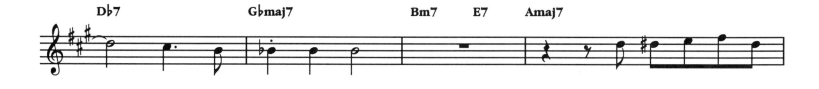

Piano Solo   **Sax Solo**   **Piano Solo**   **Bass Solo**

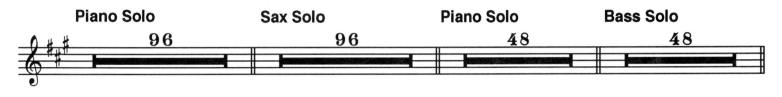

NATURE BOY

Words and Music by
EDEN AHBEZ

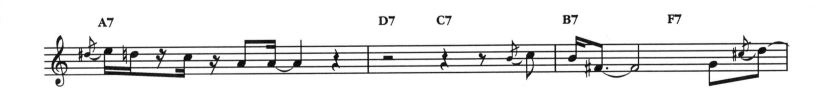

Bass Solo

Free time

IT NEVER ENTERED MY MIND

from HIGHER AND HIGHER

Words by LORENZ HART
Music by RICHARD RODGERS

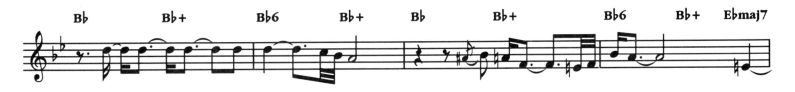

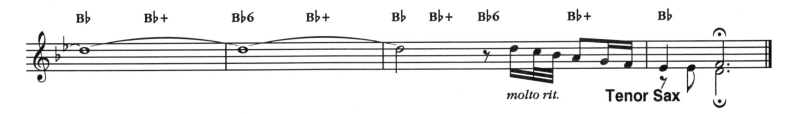

LAMENT

By J.J. JOHNSON

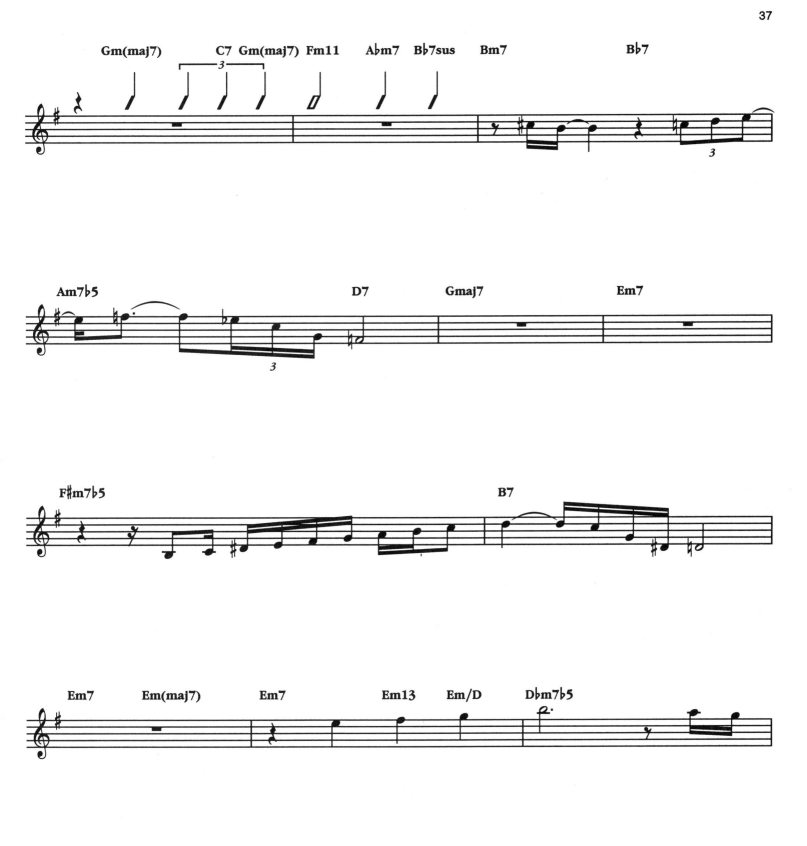

OLEO

By SONNY ROLLINS

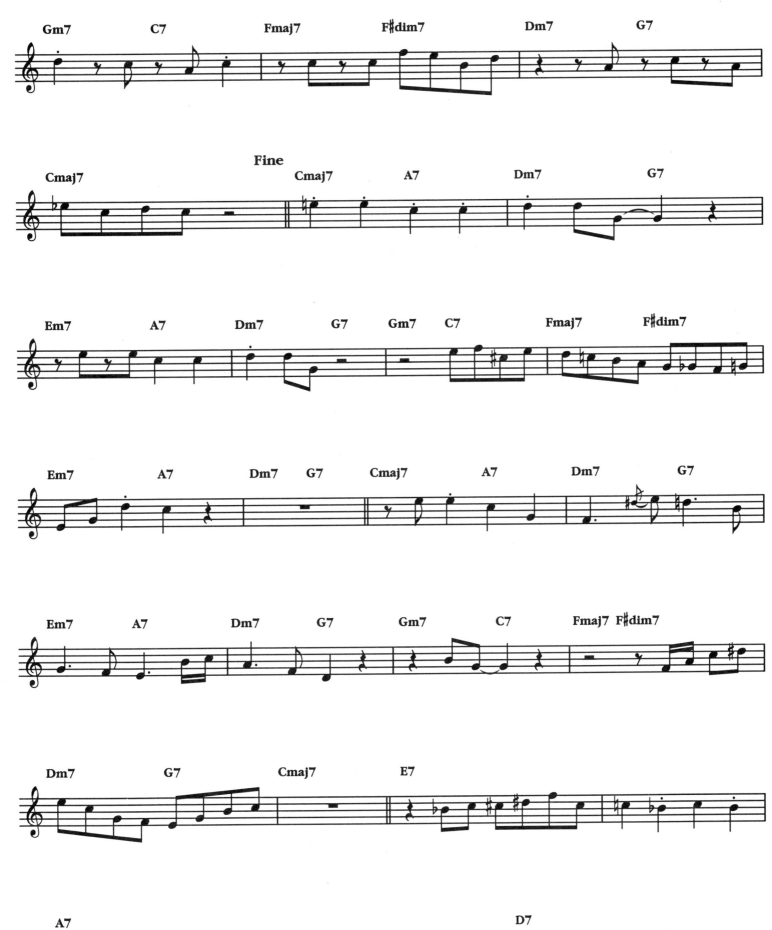

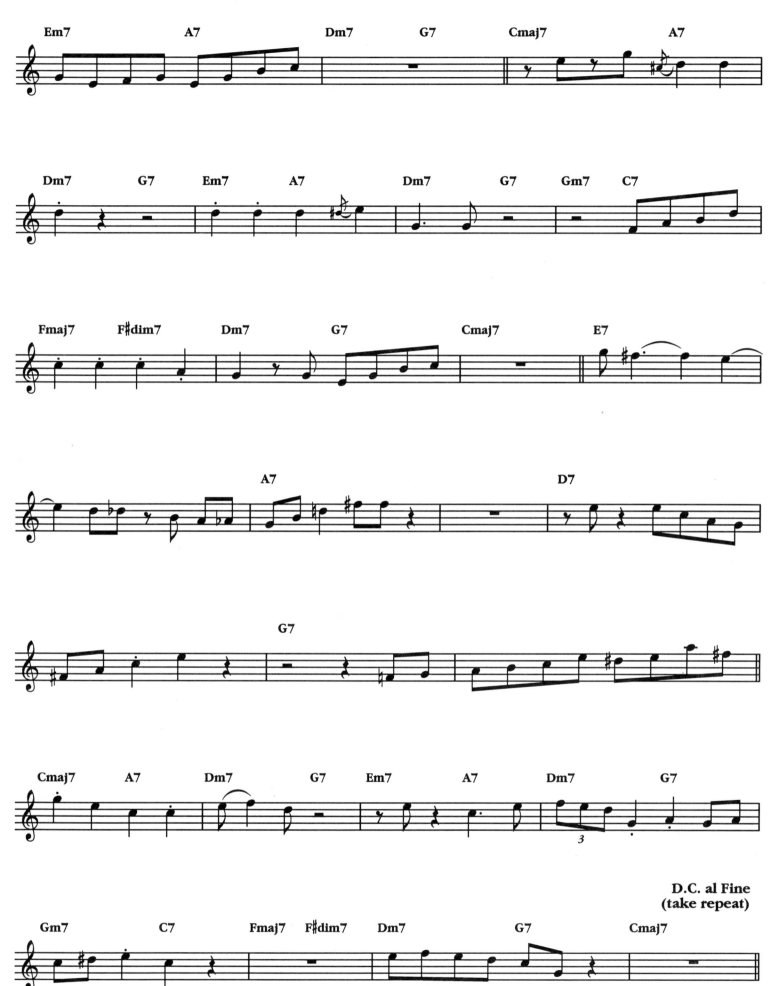

D.C. al Fine
(take repeat)

'ROUND MIDNIGHT

Words by BERNIE HANIGHEN
Music by THELONIOUS MONK and COOTIE WILLIAMS

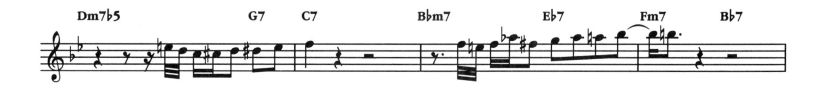

Cadenza

SOME DAY MY PRINCE WILL COME

(MASTER)

Words by LARRY MOREY
Music by FRANK CHURCHILL

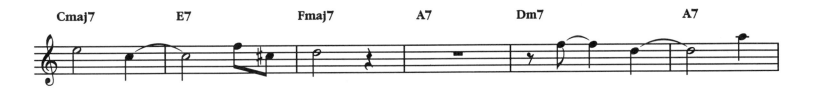

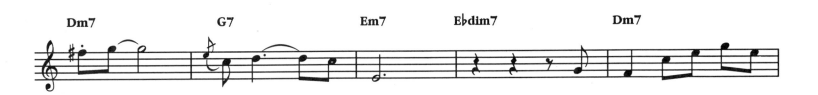

Sax Solo

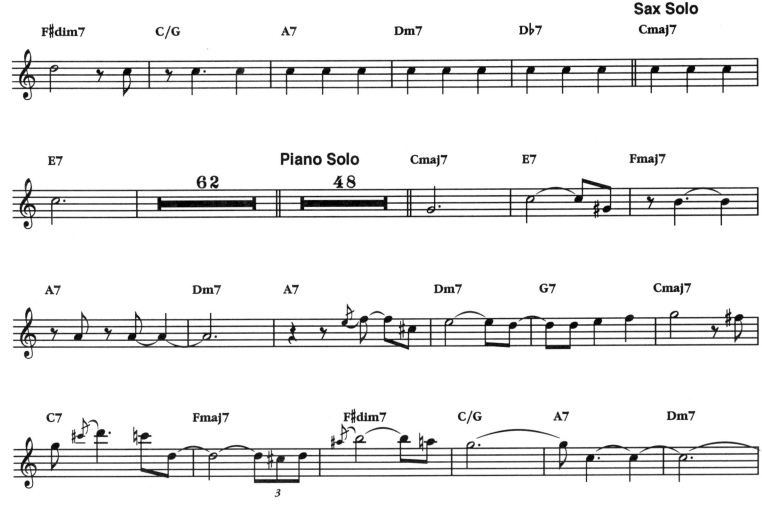

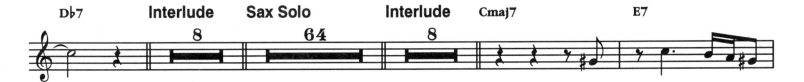

SOME DAY MY PRINCE WILL COME

(ALTERNATE TAKE)

Words by LARRY MOREY
Music by FRANK CHURCHILL

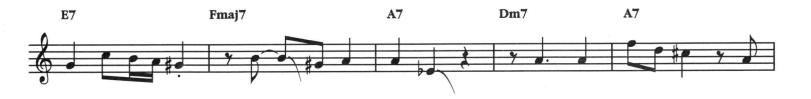

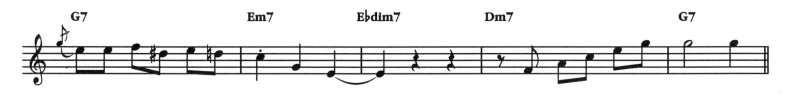

Sax Solo

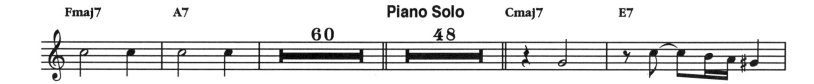

Piano Solo

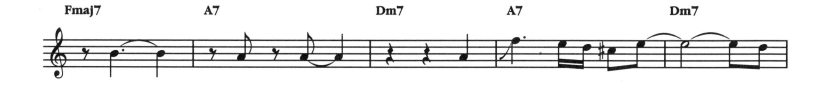

Rhythm Section

WHAT'S NEW?

Words by JOHNNY BURKE
Music by BOB HAGGART

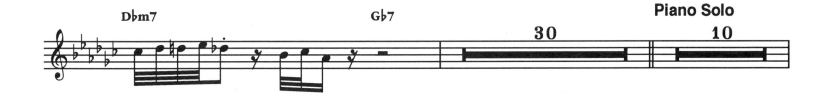

STELLA BY STARLIGHT

from the Paramount Picture THE UNINVITED

Words by NED WASHINGTON
Music by VICTOR YOUNG

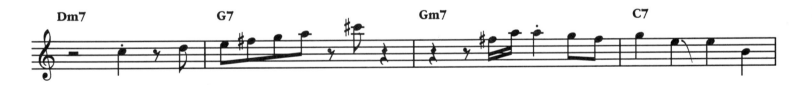

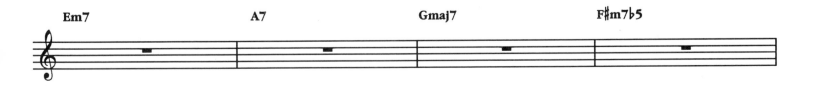

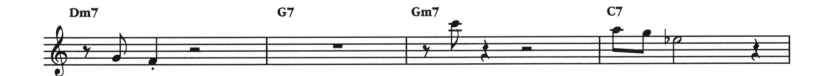

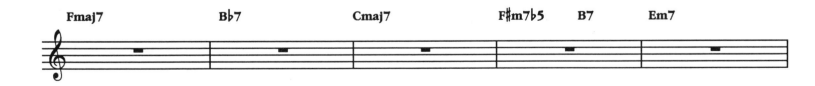

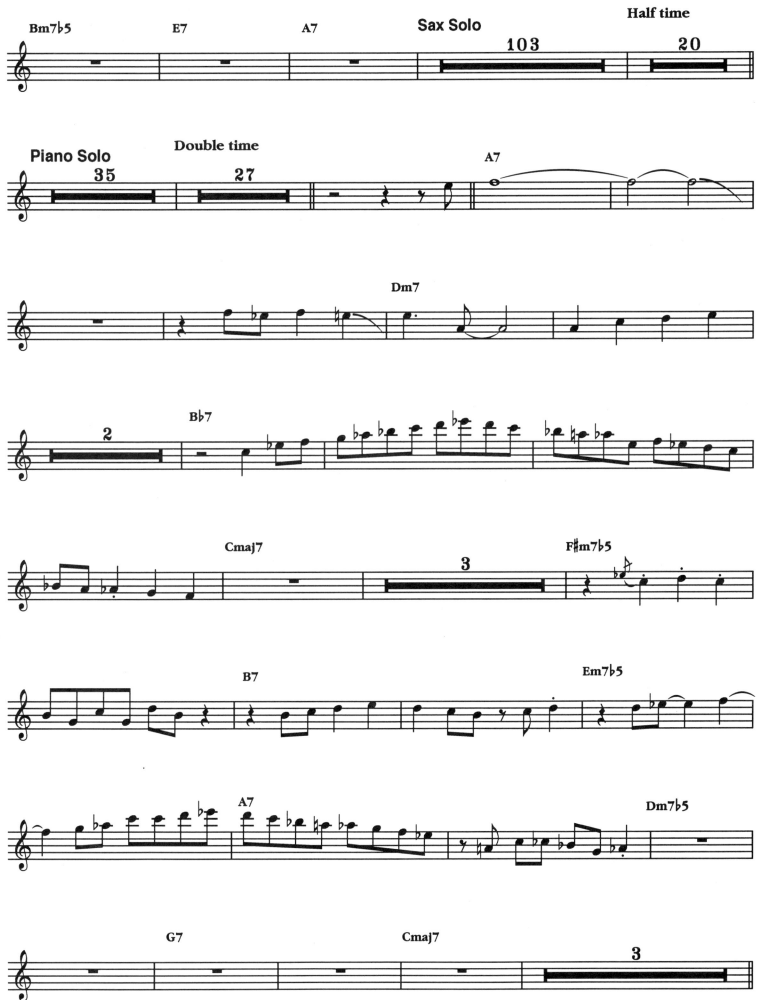

WILL YOU STILL BE MINE

Words by TOM ADAIR
Music by MATT DENNIS

G7   C7alt

Fmaj7   Cm7   F7   Bbmaj7   Bbm7

Eb7   Fmaj7   Em7b5   A7   G7   Gm7   C7

Fmaj7   Am7   D7   Gm7   C7

Fmaj7   Am7   D7   Gm7   Em7b5   A7

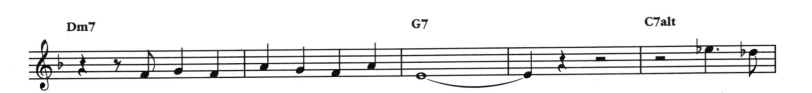

Dm7   G7   C7alt

Fmaj7   Fmaj7

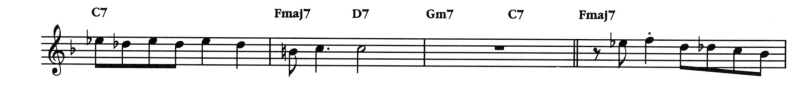

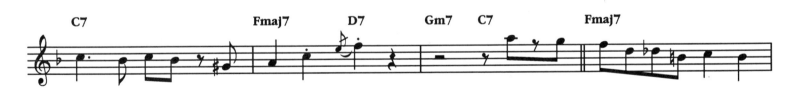

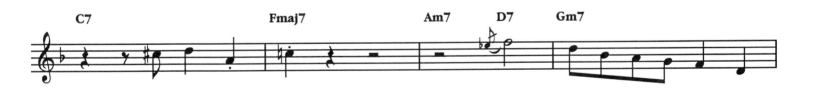

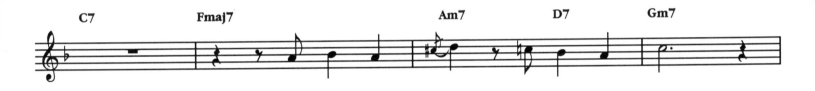

YESTERDAYS

from ROBERTA

Words by OTTO HARBACH
Music by JEROME KERN